# last-minute
# AFGHANS

Designs by Rena V. Stevens

*Annie's*™

# Introduction

Knitters of all skill levels will love this charming collection of six original designs. These projects are surprisingly easy to take with you, something you do not usually find in an afghan book. Knit in sections and worked together later, these are great projects for short amounts of downtime. Sew them together or use single crochet, add fringe or leave it off, the afghans featured here are easy to customize to suit your taste. They are made in easy-to-find yarns that are both washable and affordable. From the bold color-pop of Flamboyant Poppies to the subtle seasonal changes of Spring, Summer & Fall, these big-needle quick knits will appeal to everyone on your "to knit for" list.

Have fun knitting!

*Rena V. Stevens*

# Table of Contents

*Spring, Summer & Fall,*
**page 14**

*Prairie Impressions,*
**page 4**

*Twisted Stitches,*
**page 7**

*Candy Sprinkles,*
**page 17**

# Prairie Impressions

········································································

**Finished Measurement**
Approx 48 x 65 inches, excluding fringe

**Materials**
- Plymouth Encore Worsted Colorspun
  (worsted weight; 75% acrylic/25% wool;
  200 yds/100g per ball): 4 balls each rose
  multi #7990, blue multi #7991, rust multi #7172;
  2 balls cream multi #7718
- Plymouth Encore Worsted (worsted weight;
  75% acrylic/25% wool; 200 yds/100g per ball);
  2 balls each rose #9408, blue #598, rust #453;
  1 ball olive #45
- Size 10½ (6.5mm) needles or size needed
  to obtain gauge
- Size N/P/15 (10mm) crochet hook
- Tapestry or yarn needle

**Gauge**
11 sts = 4 inches/10cm in St st with 2 strands held tog.

To save time, take time to check gauge.

**Pattern Stitch**
**Grass Panel** (worked on 19 sts)
Panel is worked from a chart. Refer to Color Guide for background and grass color used for each panel.

**Color Guide**
**Panel A:** Make 1 using cream multi for background and olive solid for grass.
**Panel B:** Make 2 using rose multi for background and rose solid for grass.
**Panel C:** Make 2 using blue multi for background and blue solid for grass.
**Panel D:** Make 2 using rust multi for background and rust solid for grass.

## Pattern Notes
Afghan is worked in vertical panels with 2 strands of yarn held together throughout.

If only 1 ball is used, pull yarn from inside and outside of ball. When using 2 balls, pull both ends from the inside.

Slip all stitches knitwise.

Grass pattern is worked by stranding method. Do not carry yarn across more than 2 stitches on the back without catching the carried color. When changing colors, bring previous color under and over new color on wrong side to twist yarn and prevent holes.

Afghan panels can be sewn together if preferred.

## Panel
**Make 7**

*Note: Refer to Stitch Key for background and grass colors.*

With 2 strands of background color held tog, cast on 19 sts.

**Rows 1 (RS)–6:** Work Rows 1–6 of Grass Panel Chart, using indicated grass color.

**Rows 7–188:** Rep [Rows 7–20 of Grass Panel Chart] 13 times.

**Rows 189–202:** Work Rows 189–202 of Grass Panel Chart.

**Rows 203 and 204:** With background color only, rep Rows 1 and 2 of chart.

Bind off following pat for Row 1 except knit the first and last st.

## Assembly
Referring to Assembly Diagram on page 6 for placement, join panels.

Hold 2 panels WS tog with right-hand panel on top. With crochet hook and 1 strand of facing multi color, work from top to bottom of panels through both thicknesses between first and 2nd st from end of rows as follows: Leaving a 6-inch yarn end, sl st loosely in each slipped edge st across. Fasten off, leaving a 6-inch length of yarn. With yarn ends, sew ends of seams tog.

## Fringe (optional)

Use 10 (16-inch) strands per knot. Place knots evenly spaced across each short end having 1 solid motif color knot at each end of each grass motif, 1 multi color knot at edge of St st area of each panel, and 1 multi fringe at each outer corner. ●

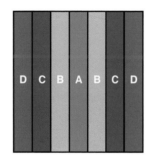

**ASSEMBLY DIAGRAM**

D | C | B | A | B | C | D

**STITCH KEY**
- ☐ K on RS, p on WS in background color
- ■ K on RS, p on WS in grass color
- − P on RS, k on WS in background color
- ⊽ Sl 1 kwise

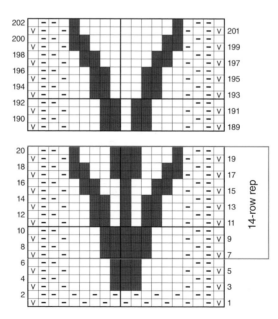

**GRASS PANEL CHART**

14-row rep

# Twisted Stitches

**Finished Measurements**
Approx 53 x 67 inches

**Materials**
- Lion Brand Wool-Ease (worsted weight; 80% acrylic/20% wool; 197 yds/85g per ball): 5 balls each blush heather #104 (A), wheat #402 (B) and chestnut heather #179 (C); 4 balls rose heather #140 (D); 3 balls mushroom #403 (E)
- Size 11 (8mm) needles or size needed to obtain gauge
- Size N/P/15 (10mm) crochet hook

**Gauge**
11 sts = 4 inches/10cm in St st with 2 strands of yarn held tog.

To save time, take time to check gauge.

**Special Abbreviations**
**Left Twist (LT):** Skip first st on LH needle, knit through back loop of 2nd st leaving both sts on needle, then insert needle into back loops of both sts and k2tog; slip both sts from needle tog.

**Right Twist (RT):** K2tog, leaving both sts on LH needle, insert RH needle from front between these 2 sts and knit the first st again; slip both sts from needle tog.

**Pattern Notes**
Afghan is worked in vertical panels with 2 strands of yarn held together.

Slip all stitches knitwise.

When using 2 balls of yarn, pull both ends from the inside. If using only 1 ball, pull one end from the inside and one from outside.

Afghan can be assembled by sewing panels together, if preferred with a decorative chain stitch added between the panels.

Panels will be longer than finished length until assembly is completed.

Charts are included for each panel for those preferring to work panel patterns from a chart.

**Panel #1**
**Make 1**

With 2 strands D held tog, cast on 28 sts.

**Row 1 (WS):** Sl 1, k3, *p1, k1; rep from * to last 6 sts, p1, k4, sl 1.

**Row 2 (RS):** P4, [LT, k2] twice, LT, [RT, k2] twice, RT, p4.

**Row 3:** Sl 1, k4, p18, k4, sl 1.

**Row 4:** P5, [LT, k2] twice, [RT, k2] twice, RT, p5.

**Row 5:** Sl 1, k5, p16, k5, sl 1.

**Row 6:** P6, LT, k2, [LT, RT] twice, k2, RT, p6.

**Row 7:** Sl 1, k6, p14, k6, sl 1.

**Row 8:** P7, [LT, k2] 3 times, RT, p7.

**Row 9:** Sl 1, k7, p12, k7, sl 1.

**Row 10:** P8, [LT, RT] 3 times, p8.

**Row 11:** Sl 1, k8, p10, k8, sl 1.

**Row 12:** P9, [RT, k2] twice, RT, p9.

**Row 13:** Rep Row 11.

**Row 14:** P8, [RT, LT] 3 times, p8.

**Row 15:** Rep Row 9.

**Row 16:** P7, RT, k2, [LT, k2] twice, LT, p7.

**Row 17:** Rep Row 7.

**Row 18:** P6, RT, k2, [RT, LT] twice, k2, LT, p6.

**Row 19:** Rep Row 5.

**Row 20:** P5, [RT, k2] 3 times, LT, k2, LT, p5.

**Row 21:** Rep Row 3.

**Row 22:** P4, [RT, k2] twice, RT, [LT, k2] twice, LT, p4.

**Row 23:** Sl 1, k3, p20, k3, sl 1.

**Row 24:** P4, [k1-tbl, k3] twice, k1-tbl, k2, [k1-tbl, k3] twice, k1-tbl, p4.

**Row 25:** Rep Row 23.

Rep [Rows 2–25] 8 times more.

Rep Rows 2–24 once—240 rows.

Bind off following Row 1 pat and knitting first and last st.

### Panel #2
**Make 2**

With 2 strands B held tog, cast on 18.

**Row 1 (WS):** Sl 1, k3, *p1, k1; rep from * to last 6 sts, p1, k4, sl 1.

**Row 2 (RS):** P4, LT, [k2, RT] twice, p4.

**Row 3:** Sl 1, k4, p8, k4, sl 1.

**Row 4:** P5, [LT, RT] twice, p5.

**Row 5:** Sl 1, k5, p6, k5, sl 1.

**Row 6:** P6, RT, k2, RT, p6.

**Row 7:** Rep Row 5.

**Row 8:** P5, [RT, LT] twice, p5.

**Row 9:** Rep Row 3.

**Row 10:** P4, [RT, k2] twice, LT, p4.

**Row 11:** Sl 1, k3, p10, k3, sl 1.

**Row 12:** P4, k1-tbl, k3, [k1-tbl] twice, k3, k1-tbl, p4.

**Row 13:** Rep Row 11.

Rep [Rows 2–13] 18 times more.

Rep Rows 2–12 once—240 rows.

Bind off following Row 1 except knitting the first and last sts.

### Panel #3
**Make 2**

With 2 strands E held tog, cast on 12.

**Row 1 (WS):** Sl 1, k3, p1, k1, p1, k4, sl 1.

**Row 2 (RS):** P4, LT, RT, p4.

**Row 3:** Sl 1, k4, p2, k4, sl 1.

**Row 4:** P5, RT, p5.

**Rows 5 and 6:** Rep Rows 3 and 4.

**Row 7:** Rep Row 3.

**Row 8:** P4, RT, LT, p4.

**Row 9:** Sl 1, k3, p4, k3, sl 1.

Rep [Rows 2–9] 28 times more.

Rep Rows 2–8 once—240 rows.

Bind off as for Row 1 except knit first and last st.

### Panel #4
**Make 2**

With 2 strands A held tog, cast on 20.

**Row 1 (WS):** Sl 1, k4, *p1, k1; rep from * to last 7 sts, p1, k5, sl 1.

**Row 2 (RS):** P4, [RT, LT] 3 times, p4.

**Row 3:** Sl 1, k3, p12, k3, sl 1.

**Row 4:** P4, k1-tbl, [k2, LT] twice, k2, k1-tbl, p4.

**Row 5:** Rep Row 3.

**Row 6:** P4, [LT, RT] 3 times, p4.

**Row 7:** Sl 1, k4, p10, k4, sl 1.

**Row 8:** P5, [RT, k2] twice, RT, p5.

**Row 9:** Rep Row 7.

Rep [Rows 2–9] 28 times more.

Rep Rows 2–8 once—240 rows.

Bind off as for Row 1 except knit first and last st.

### Panel #5
**Make 2**

*Note: Moss sts background helps prevent curling along edges.*

With 2 strands C held tog, cast on 16.

**Row 1 (WS):** Sl 1, *k1, p1; rep from * to last st, sl 1.

**Row 2 (RS):** P2, k1, p4, RT, p4, k1, p2.

**Row 3:** Sl 1, p1, k1, p1, k3, p2, k3, p1, k1, p1, sl 1.

**Row 4:** P2, k1, p3, RT, LT, p3, k1, p2.

**Row 5:** Sl 1, p1, k1, p1, k2, p4, k2, p1, k1, p1, sl 1.

**Row 6:** P2, k1, p3, k1-tbl, k2, k1-tbl, p3, k1, p2.

## Fringe

Use 9 (16-inch) strands per knot. With same color as panel, place 1 knot at each joining stripe and 1 knot at center of each panel across top and bottom end of afghan. ●

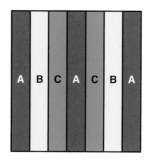

**ASSEMBLY DIAGRAM**

# Spring, Summer & Fall

## Skill Level

■ ■ □ □ EASY

## Finished Measurements

Approx 42 x 63 inches, excluding fringe

## Materials

- Berroco Comfort (worsted weight; 50% super fine nylon/50% super fine acrylic; 210 yds/100g per ball): 3 balls each Adirondack #9752 (A), lovage #9761 (B), Aunt Martha green #9748 (C), lidfors #9764 (D), kidz orange #9731 (E), spice #9765 (F), beet root #9760 (G)
- Size 13 (9mm) needles or size needed to obtain gauge
- Size N/P/15 (10mm) crochet hook

## Gauge

8 sts = 4 inches/10cm in St st with 3 strands of yarn held tog.

To save time, take time to check gauge.

## Special Abbreviations

**Double yarn over (2yo):** Wrap yarn twice around needle. On next row, purl in first loop, slipping both loops off LH needle.

*Note: 2yo on working row counts as 1 st.*

**Slip, ssk, psso (sl-ssk-psso):** Sl 1 pwise, ssk over next 2 sts, pass slipped st over st resulting from ssk—2 sts dec.

## Pattern Notes

Worked in vertical panels holding 3 strands together. Be sure to check gauge. If using a yarn other than the one suggested, only 2 strands may be needed to achieve gauge.

Afghan can be assembled by sewing panels together, if preferred.

## Leaf Panel

**Make 1 panel in each color**

*Notes: Stitch count increases by 1 on Row 1 and is restored to the original count on Row 5.*

*A chart is provided for those preferring to work panel pat from a chart.*

With 3 strands held tog, loosely cast on 13 sts.

**Row 1 (RS):** K1, p1, k1-tbl, 2yo, k5, 2yo, ssk, k1, p1, k1—14 sts.

Mark Row 1 as bottom edge and RS of Panel.

*Note: Purl into first loop of 2yo, dropping both loops from needle.*

**Row 2 and all WS rows:** P1, k1, purl to last 2 sts, k1, p1.

**Row 3:** K1, p1, k1-tbl, 2yo, k1, ssk, k1, k2tog, k1, 2yo, k2, p1, k1.

**Row 5:** K1, p1, k1-tbl, 2yo, k1, ssk, k1, k2tog, k1, 2yo, k2tog, p1, k1—13 sts.

**Row 7:** K1, p1, [k1-tbl, 2yo] twice, ssk, k1, k2tog, 2yo, k2tog, p1, k1.

**Row 9:** K1, p1, k1-tbl, 2yo, k3, 2yo, sl-ssk-psso, 2yo, k2tog, p1, k1.

Rep [Rows 1–10] 14 times more.

Bind off on RS as follows: K1, p1, knit to last 2 sts, p1, k1.

## Assembly

Arrange Panels as shown in Assembly Diagram.

Hold 2 panels with WS tog, right-hand panel facing. Beg at lower edge, with crochet hook and 1 strand of facing color, work from top to bottom of Panels through both thicknesses between first and 2nd st from end of rows as follows: Leaving approx 6-inch length of yarn, join yarn with sl st in first row of facing Panel and in 5th row of back Panel. Sl st loosely in next and each row through last row of back Panel, leaving last rows of facing Panel unworked; fasten off, leaving approx 6-inch length of yarn at end. With yarn ends, loosely sew ends of seam to secure before weaving in; finish off.

## Fringe

Using 12 (16-inch) strands per knot and matching colors, place 1 knot at each point along top and bottom end, 1 evenly spaced between, and 1 at each rem outer afghan corner. ●

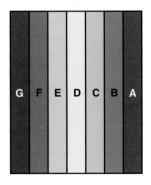

**ASSEMBLY DIAGRAM**

**STITCH KEY**

- ☐ K on RS, p on WS
- ⊟ P on RS, k on WS
- ☒ K1-tbl on RS, p1-tbl on WS
- ◺ Ssk
- ◹ K2tog
- ② 2yo
- ⋉ Sl-ssk-psso on RS
- ▨ No stitch

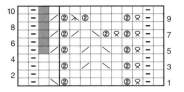

**LEAF PANEL CHART**

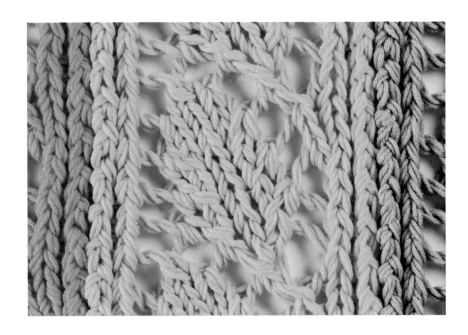

# Candy Sprinkles

## Finished Measurements
Approx 40 x 51 inches

## Materials
- Lion Brand Hometown USA (super bulky; 94% acrylic/6% rayon; 64 yds/113g per ball): 7 balls Virginia Beach #214 (MC)
- Lion Brand Hometown USA (super bulky; 100% acrylic; 81 yds/140g per ball): 1 ball each Detroit blue #105, Cincinnati red #113, Minneapolis purple #147, Green Bay #130, Pittsburgh yellow #158, Syracuse orange #133, Honolulu pink #102
- Size 13 (9mm) needles or size needed to obtain gauge
- Size N/P/15 (10mm) crochet hook

**6 SUPER BULKY**

## Gauge
11 sts = 6 inches in double moss st.

To save time, take time to check gauge.

## Pattern Notes
Afghan is worked in vertical panels. Panels can be sewn together, if preferred.

Slip stitches knitwise with yarn in back.

## Panels A, C & E
With MC, cast on 15 sts.

### Double Moss Rectangle
**Row 1 (RS):** Sl 1, knit to last st, sl 1.

Mark this row as bottom edge of RS of Panel.

**Row 2:** P2, *k1, p1; rep from * to last st, p1.

**Row 3:** Sl 1, *p1, k1; rep from * to last 2 sts, p1, sl 1.

**Row 4:** P1, *k1, p1; rep from * across.

**Row 5:** Sl 1, *k1, p1; rep from * to last 2 sts, k1, sl 1.

**Rows 6–9:** Rep Rows 2–5.

**Rows 10–12:** Rep Rows 2–4.

### Lace Rectangle
*Note: Refer to Color and Assembly Diagram for color sequence in each panel.*

**Row 13:** With indicated color, sl 1, k1, *yo, k2tog; rep from * across to last st, sl 1.

**Row 14:** Purl.

**Rows 15–24:** Rep [Rows 13 and 14] 5 times.

Rep Rows 1–24, continuing color sequence of appropriate panel and ending with Rows 1–12 of Double Moss rectangle.

Bind off as for Row 5 except knit first and last st.

## Panels B & D
*Note: Refer to Color and Assembly Diagram for color sequence in each panel.*

With color indicated, cast on 15 sts.

### Lace Rectangle
**Row 1 (RS):** Sl 1, *ssk, yo; rep from * to last 2 sts, k1, sl 1.

Mark this row as bottom edge of RS of panel.

**Row 2:** Purl.

**Rows 3–12:** Rep [Rows 1 and 2] 5 times.

### Double Moss Rectangle
**Row 13:** With MC, sl 1, knit to last st, sl 1.

**Row 14:** P2, *k1, p1; rep from * to last st, p1.

**Row 15:** Sl 1, *p1, k1; rep from * to last 2 sts, p1, sl 1.

**Row 16:** P1, *k1, p1; rep from * across.

**Row 17:** Sl 1, *k1, p1; rep from * to last 2 sts, k1, sl 1.

**Rows 18–21:** Rep Rows 14–17.

**Rows 22–24:** Rep Rows 14–16.

Rep Rows 1–24, continuing color sequence of appropriate panel and ending with Rows 1–12 of Lace Rectangle.

Bind off kwise.

## Assembly
Referring to Color and Assembly Diagram, place panels side by side, RS facing, left-hand edge of Panel to the right, overlapping Panel to the left and matching large (slipped) edge sts. With crochet hook and knotted loop of MC on hook, holding yarn beneath work, work loosely through both thicknesses as follows: Sl st in 1 loop only of first (cast-on) st and of each edge st across, sl st in 1 loop of bind-off row st, sl st over top. Finish off. ●

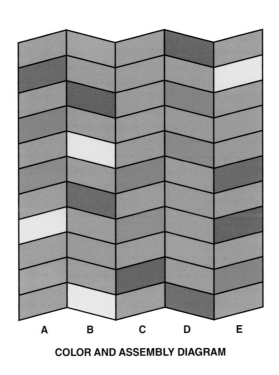

**COLOR AND ASSEMBLY DIAGRAM**

# Flamboyant Poppies

## Skill Level
 EASY

## Finished Measurements
Approx 45 x 59 inches

## Materials
- Vickie Howell for Caron Sheep(ish) (worsted weight; 70% acrylic/ 30% wool; 167 yds/85g): 4 balls yellow(ish) #0012; 3 balls each hot pink(ish) #0007, magenta(ish) #0006, turquoise(ish) #0017; 2 balls each coral(ish) #0014, teal(ish) #0016 and chartreuse(ish) #0020
- Size 11 (8mm) needles or size needed to obtain gauge
- Size N/P/15 (10mm) crochet hook

**4 MEDIUM**

## Gauge
9 sts = 4 inches in Background st with 2 strands held tog.

To save time, take time to check gauge.

## Pattern Notes
Afghan is worked in squares with 2 strands of yarn held together throughout.

Pull yarn from inside when using 2 balls together.

Afghan can be assembled and edged by sewing, if desired.

Flowers are knitted in by intarsia method. Use about 9 yards of a double strand for background at left of the flower and approximately 2 feet for the flower center. Do not carry yarn across more than 3 stitches without catching it in.

When changing colors, bring new color under and around previous color to twist yarn on wrong side and prevent holes.

Slip stitches knitwise with yarn held in back.

## Pattern Stitch
### Background

**Row 1 (RS):** Sl 1 kwise, *k1, p1; rep from * to last 2 sts, k1, sl 1 kwise.

**Row 2:** Purl the knit sts and slip sts and knit the purl sts.

Rep Row 2, slipping the first and last st of RS rows.

## Square
### Make 20

Refer to Color and Assembly Diagram for flower and background color for each square.

With 2 strands of background color held tog, cast on 25 sts.

**Rows 1–6:** Referring to Poppy Chart, work Rows 1–6 in Background pat.

**Rows 7–37:** Continuing in established pat for background and changing colors as indicated for flower, work rem rows of Poppy Chart.

Bind off in pat.

## Assembly
Place squares according to Color and Assembly Diagram. Join squares into vertical panels as follows: With squares side by side and RS facing, place knotted loop of 2 strands of chartreuse on hook; holding yarn beneath work, and working loosely in both loops (4 strands) of bottom and top edge sts, respectively, sl st in first st of right-hand square, sl st in first st of left-hand square, sl st again in same st as beg sl st, *on left-hand square, skip next st, sl st in next st, on right-hand square, skip next st, sl st in next st; rep from * across through working sl st in last st on each square, sl st again in same st as next-to-last sl st made; fasten off.

Join panels in same manner, working sl sts in both loops (4 strands) of each large edge st (i.e. in every 2nd row) and in end of each joining.

## Edging

With RS facing, 2 strands of chartreuse and working through both loops (4 strands) of sts; join in any outer corner, sl st, ch 1 in same corner, ch 2, sl st in first and every 2nd st across top and bottom ends and ch 3, sl st in first and every 2nd large edge st across side edges; work (sl st, ch 4, sl st) in each corner, joining with sl st in beg ch after working ch-4 in last corner. Finish off. ●

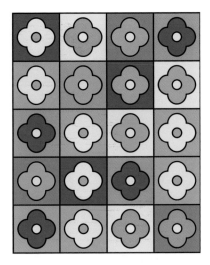

**COLOR AND ASSEMBLY DIAGRAM**

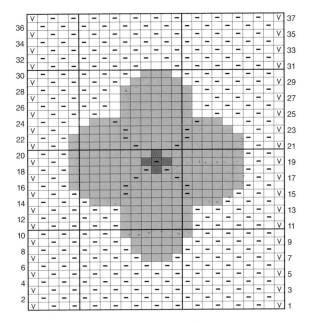

**POPPY CHART**

**COLOR KEY**
- ☐ Yellow(ish)
- ☐ Hot pink(ish)
- ☐ Magenta(ish)
- ☐ Turquoise(ish)
- ☐ Coral(ish)
- ☐ Teal(ish)

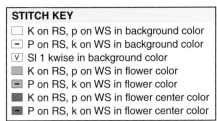

**STITCH KEY**
- ☐ K on RS, p on WS in background color
- – P on RS, k on WS in background color
- ☑ Sl 1 kwise in background color
- ☐ K on RS, p on WS in flower color
- – P on RS, k on WS in flower color
- ☐ K on RS, p on WS in flower center color
- – P on RS, k on WS in flower center color

# General Information

## Abbreviations & Symbols

**[ ]** work instructions within brackets as many times as directed

**( )** work instructions within parentheses in the place directed

**\*\*** repeat instructions following the asterisks as directed

**\*** repeat instructions following the single asterisk as directed

**"** inch(es)

**approx** approximately
**beg** begin/begins/beginning
**CC** contrasting color
**ch** chain stitch
**cm** centimeter(s)
**cn** cable needle
**dec(s)** decrease/decreases/decreasing
**dpn(s)** double-point needle(s)
**g** gram(s)
**inc(s)** increase/increases/increasing

**k** knit
**k2tog** knit 2 stitches together
**kfb** knit in front and back
**kwise** knitwise
**LH** left hand
**m** meter(s)
**M1** make one stitch
**MC** main color
**mm** millimeter(s)
**oz** ounce(s)
**p** purl
**p2tog** purl 2 stitches together
**pat(s)** pattern(s)
**pm** place marker
**psso** pass slipped stitch over
**pwise** purlwise
**rem** remain/remains/remaining
**rep(s)** repeat(s)
**rev St st** reverse stockinette stitch
**RH** right hand
**rnd(s)** rounds
**RS** right side

**skp** slip, knit, pass slipped stitch over—1 stitch decreased
**sk2p** slip 1, knit 2 together, pass slipped stitch over the knit 2 together—2 stitches decreased
**sl** slip
**sl 1 kwise** slip 1 knitwise
**sl 1 pwise** slip 1 purlwise
**sl st** slip stitch(es)
**ssk** slip, slip, knit these 2 stitches together—a decrease
**st(s)** stitch(es)
**St st** stockinette stitch
**tbl** through back loop(s)
**tog** together
**WS** wrong side
**wyib** with yarn in back
**wyif** with yarn in front
**yd(s)** yard(s)
**yfwd** yarn forward
**yo (yo's)** yarn over(s)

## Skill Levels

**BEGINNER**

Beginner projects for first-time knitters using basic stitches. Minimal shaping.

**EASY**

Easy projects using basic stitches, repetitive stitch patterns, simple color changes and simple shaping and finishing.

**INTERMEDIATE**

Intermediate projects with a variety of stitches, mid-level shaping and finishing.

**EXPERIENCED**

Experienced projects using advanced techniques and stitches, detailed shaping and refined finishing.

## Standard Yarn Weight System
Categories of yarn, gauge ranges and recommended needle sizes.

| Yarn Weight Symbol & Category Names | 1 SUPER FINE | 2 FINE | 3 LIGHT | 4 MEDIUM | 5 BULKY | 6 SUPER BULKY |
|---|---|---|---|---|---|---|
| **Type of Yarns in Category** | Sock, Fingering, Baby | Sport, Baby | DK, Light Worsted | Worsted, Afghan, Aran | Chunky, Craft, Rug | Bulky, Roving |
| **Knit Gauge Range* in Stockinette Stitch to 4 inches** | 27–32 sts | 23–26 sts | 21–24 sts | 16–20 sts | 12–15 sts | 6–11 sts |
| **Recommended Needle in Metric Size Range** | 2.25–3.25mm | 3.25–3.75mm | 3.75–4.5mm | 4.5–5.5mm | 5.5–8mm | 8mm and larger |
| **Recommended Needle U.S. Size Range** | 1 to 3 | 3 to 5 | 5 to 7 | 7 to 9 | 9 to 11 | 11 and larger |

**\* GUIDELINES ONLY:** The above reflect the most commonly used gauges and needle sizes for specific yarn categories.

## Inches Into Millimeters & Centimeters
All measurements are rounded off slightly.

| inches | mm | cm | inches | cm | inches | cm | inches | cm |
|---|---|---|---|---|---|---|---|---|
| ⅛ | 3 | 0.3 | 5 | 12.5 | 21 | 53.5 | 38 | 96.5 |
| ¼ | 6 | 0.6 | 5½ | 14 | 22 | 56.0 | 39 | 99.0 |
| ⅜ | 10 | 1.0 | 6 | 15.0 | 23 | 58.5 | 40 | 101.5 |
| ½ | 13 | 1.3 | 7 | 18.0 | 24 | 61.0 | 41 | 104.0 |
| ⅝ | 15 | 1.5 | 8 | 20.5 | 25 | 63.5 | 42 | 106.5 |
| ¾ | 20 | 2.0 | 9 | 23.0 | 26 | 66.0 | 43 | 109.0 |
| ⅞ | 22 | 2.2 | 10 | 25.5 | 27 | 68.5 | 44 | 112.0 |
| 1 | 25 | 2.5 | 11 | 28.0 | 28 | 71.0 | 45 | 114.5 |
| 1¼ | 32 | 3.2 | 12 | 30.5 | 29 | 73.5 | 46 | 117.0 |
| 1½ | 38 | 3.8 | 13 | 33.0 | 30 | 76.0 | 47 | 119.5 |
| 1¾ | 45 | 4.5 | 14 | 35.5 | 31 | 79.0 | 48 | 122.0 |
| 2 | 50 | 5.0 | 15 | 38.0 | 32 | 81.5 | 49 | 124.5 |
| 2½ | 65 | 6.5 | 16 | 40.5 | 33 | 84.0 | 50 | 127.0 |
| 3 | 75 | 7.5 | 17 | 43.0 | 34 | 86.5 | | |
| 3½ | 90 | 9.0 | 18 | 46.0 | 35 | 89.0 | | |
| 4 | 100 | 10.0 | 19 | 48.5 | 36 | 91.5 | | |
| 4½ | 115 | 11.5 | 20 | 51.0 | 37 | 94.0 | | |

# Knitting Basics

## Cast-On

Leaving an end about an inch long for each stitch to be cast on, make a slip knot on the right needle.

Place the thumb and index finger of your left hand between the yarn ends with the long yarn end over your thumb, and the strand from the skein over your index finger. Close your other fingers over the strands to hold them against your palm. Spread your thumb and index fingers apart and draw the yarn into a "V."

Place the needle in front of the strand around your thumb and bring it underneath this strand. Carry the needle over and under the strand on your index finger.

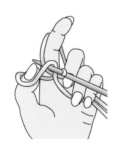

Draw through loop on thumb.

Drop the loop from your thumb and draw up the strand to form a stitch on the needle.

Repeat until you have cast on the number of stitches indicated in the pattern. Remember to count the beginning slip knot as a stitch.

## Knit (K)

Insert tip of right needle from front to back in next stitch on left needle.

Bring yarn under and over the tip of the right needle.

Pull yarn loop through the stitch with right needle point.

Slide the stitch off the left needle. The new stitch is on the right needle.

## Purl (P)

With yarn in front, insert tip of right needle from back to front through next stitch on the left needle.

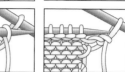

Bring yarn around the right needle counterclockwise. With right needle, draw yarn back through the stitch.

Slide the stitch off the left needle.

The new stitch is on the right needle.

## Bind-Off

### Binding Off (Knit)

Knit first two stitches on left needle. Insert tip of left needle into first stitch worked on right needle and pull it over the second stitch and completely off the needle.

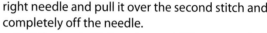

Knit the next stitch and repeat. When one stitch remains on right needle, cut yarn and draw tail through last stitch to fasten off.

### Binding Off (Purl)

Purl first two stitches on left needle. Insert tip of left needle into first stitch worked on right needle and pull it over the second stitch and completely off the needle.

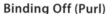

Purl the next stitch and repeat. When one stitch remains on right needle, cut yarn and draw tail through last stitch to fasten off.

## Invisible Increase (M1)

There are several ways to make or increase one stitch.

### Make 1 With Left Twist (M1L)

Insert left needle from front to back under the horizontal loop between the last stitch worked and next stitch on left needle.

With right needle, knit into the back of this loop.

To make this increase on the purl side, insert left needle in same manner and purl into the back of the loop.

## Make 1 With Right Twist (M1R)

Insert left needle from back to front under the horizontal loop between the last stitch worked and next stitch on left needle.

With right needle, knit into the front of this loop.

To make this increase on the purl side, insert left needle in same manner and purl into the front of the loop.

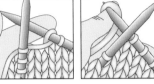

## Make 1 With Backward Loop Over the Right Needle

With your thumb, make a loop over the right needle.

Slip the loop from your thumb onto the needle and pull to tighten.

## Make 1 in Top of Stitch Below

Insert tip of right needle into the stitch on left needle one row below.

Knit this stitch, then knit the stitch on the left needle.

## Decrease (Dec)

### Knit 2 Together (K2tog)

Put tip of right needle through next two stitches on left needle as to knit. Knit these two stitches as one.

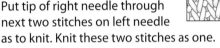

### Purl 2 Together (P2tog)

Put tip of right needle through next two stitches on left needle as to purl. Purl these two stitches as one.

### Slip, Slip, Knit (Ssk)

Slip next two stitches, one at a time as to knit, from left needle to right needle.

Insert left needle in front of both stitches and knit them together.

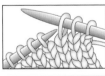

## Fringe Instructions

### Basic Instructions

Cut a piece of cardboard half as long as specified in instructions for strands plus ½ inch for trimming allowance. Wind yarn loosely and evenly lengthwise around cardboard. When card is filled, cut yarn across one end. Do this several times, and then begin fringing; you can wind additional strands as you need them.

### Single-Knot Fringe

Hold specified number of strands for one knot of fringe together, and then fold in half. Hold afghan with right side facing you. Use crochet hook to draw folded end through space or stitch from right to wrong side (Figures 1 and 2), pull loose ends through folded section (Figure 3) and draw knot up firmly (Figure 4). Space knots as indicated in pattern instructions.

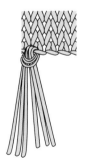

**Figure 1**

**Figure 2**

**Figure 3**

**Figure 4**

# Crochet Stitches

## Chain (Ch)
Yarn over, pull through loop on hook.

**Chain Stitch**

## Slip Stitch (Sl St)
Insert hook under both loops of the stitch, bring yarn over the hook from back to front and draw it through the stitch and the loop on the hook.

**Slip Stitch**

## Slip Stitch Seam
Creates a bulky seam. Place slip knot on hook, holding two pieces with right sides facing, slip stitch through top loops of corresponding pieces. For a firmer seam, slip stitch through both top loops. To add a ridged design element, slip stitch together with wrong sides facing so seam is on outside of garment.

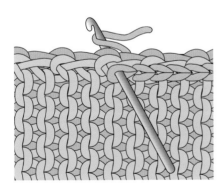

**Slip Stitch Seam**

## Single Crochet (Sc)
Insert the hook in the second chain through the center of the V. Bring the yarn over the hook from back to front.

Draw the yarn through the chain stitch and onto the hook.

Again bring yarn over the hook from back to front and draw it through both loops on hook.

For additional rows of single crochet, insert the hook under both loops of the previous stitch instead of through the center of the V as when working into the chain stitch.

**Single Crochet**

# Stitch & Color Techniques

. . . . . . . . . . . . . . . . . . . . . . . . . . . . . . . . . . . . . . . . . . . . . . . . . . . . . . . . . . . . . .

### Working From Charts

When working with more than one color in a row or round, sometimes a chart is provided to follow the pattern. On the chart each square represents one stitch. A key is given indicating the color or stitch represended by each color or symbol in the box.

When working in rows, right-side rows are read from right to left, and wrong-side rows are read from left to right.

### Stranded or Fair Isle Knitting

Changing colors of yarn within the round or row is called Stranded, or Fair Isle, knitting. This type of knitting can be worked either with both yarns in one hand, as shown in the photo to the right, or with one yarn in each hand. Carry the yarns along the wrong side of the fabric, working each color in the order indicated by the pattern. One color should always be carried under the other, whether you are knitting or purling—the strands will run parallel on the wrong side, as shown below. They should never change positions; if they do, it will be apparent on the right side of the fabric. If working back and forth, carry both yarns to the end of each row and twist to "lock" them in position on the last stitch.

When one of the yarns is carried across the back for more than 5 stitches (or about an inch), the yarn should be caught into the back of one of the stitches that is worked with the other yarn. This will prevent snags caused by long floats.

Stranded colorwork knitting creates a denser fabric than plain Stockinette knitting. Always work your gauge swatch in pattern before beginning your project. Watch your tension, ensuring that the stranded yarn is not pulled too tight; this will create puckers on the front of the fabric.

## Intarsia

In certain patterns there are larger areas of color within the piece. Since this type of pattern requires a new color only for that section, it is not necessary to carry the yarn back and forth across the back. For this type of color change, a separate ball of yarn or bobbin is used for each section of color, making the yarn available only where needed.

Before beginning the project, wind a bobbin for each color area, allowing ¾ inch for each stitch plus 10 inches extra to weave in at beginning and end of color section.

Bring the new yarn being used up and around the yarn just worked; this will twist, or "lock" the colors and prevent holes from occurring at the join. The two bottom photos show how the two colors are twisted together on the wrong side of the work. ●

# Resources

**Berroco Inc.**
1 Tupperware Drive, Suite 4
N. Smithfield, RI 02896-6815
(401) 769-1212
www.berroco.com

**Lion Brand Yarn**
135 Kero Road
Carlstadt, NJ 07072
(800) 258-9276
www.lionbrand.com

**Plymouth Yarn Co.**
500 Lafayette St.
Box 28
Bristol, PA 19007-0028
(215) 788-0459
www.plymouthyarn.com

**Spinrite Inc.**
**(Caron)**
320 Livingstone Ave. South
Box 40
Listowel, ON
N4W 3H3 Canada
(800) 811-2325
www.caron.com

**Universal Yarn Inc.**
5991 Caldwell Business Park Drive
Harrisburg, NC 28075
(704) 789-YARN (9276)
www.universalyarn.com

# Meet the Designer

Born in the Netherlands, Rena V. Stevens says her knitting memories are of Wednesday afternoons when the boys were out playing, while the girls had to stay in school to learn needlecrafts. Rena's family moved briefly to Canada before finally settling in California. Crafting through it all, she progressed from doll clothes to dog harnesses to sweaters.

Rena's designing career has provided her with joy and recreation ever since selling her first design in 1988. During her days as a college professor, designing was the perfect complement to her career. During the school year, Stevens would always find spare time to work up swatches and envision new designs.

Afghans are her absolute favorite and she has sold more than 150 designs and authored 15 books. Rena lives in Escondido, Calif., with her husband, Steve. She has a daughter, Claire; a grandson, Asher; a dog, Pheobe; and three cats. Rena retired from teaching almost four years ago but as anyone who is having a good retirement will tell you, she's still as busy as ever! ●

# Photo Index

4

12

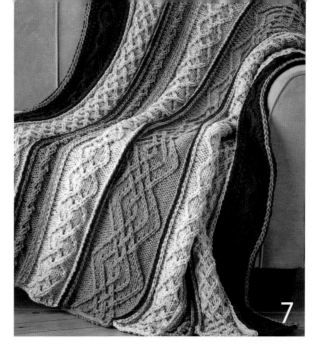

7

14

20

17

 *Last-Minute Afghans* is published by Annie's, 306 East Parr Road, Berne, IN 46711. Printed in USA. Copyright © 2012 Annie's. All rights reserved. This publication may not be reproduced in part or in whole without written permission from the publisher.

**RETAIL STORES:** If you would like to carry this pattern book or any other Annie's publication, visit AnniesWSL.com.

Every effort has been made to ensure that the instructions in this pattern book are complete and accurate. We cannot, however, take responsibility for human error, typographical mistakes or variations in individual work. Please visit AnniesCustomerCare.com to check for pattern updates.

ISBN: 978-1-59635-607-8

2 3 4 5 6 7 8 9